Adorn

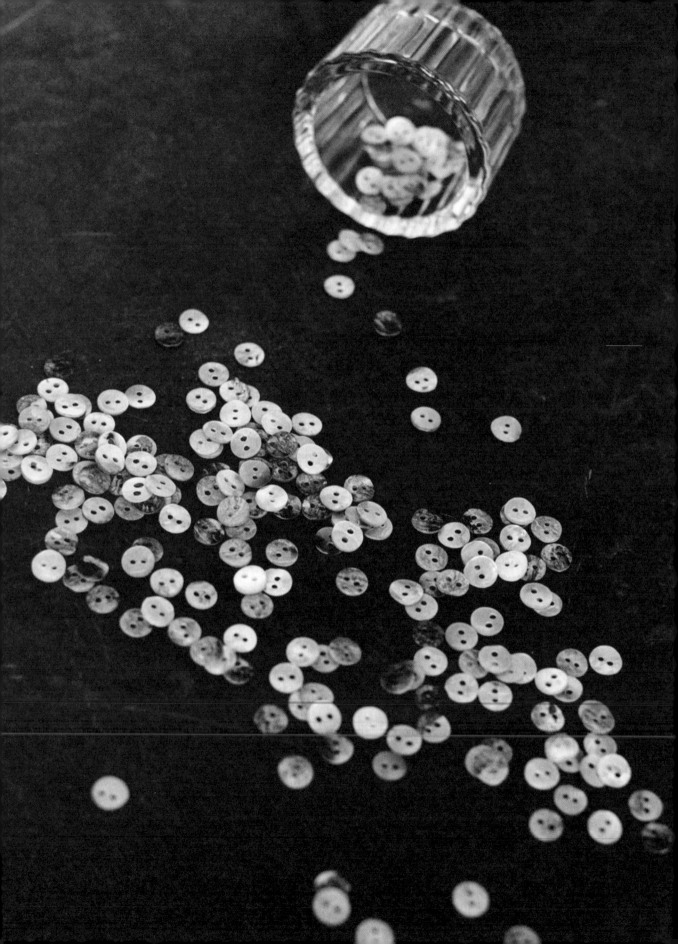

Adorn

25 STYLISH
DIY FASHION PROJECTS

KIT LEE & SHINI PARK

hardie grant books
MELBOURNE · LONDON

CONTENTS

Like all good ideas, it started over brunch...

The first time I met Kit, we were sitting diagonally across from one another, cradling a latte each. We waved our hellos and threw our names across the long table. It was the first ever blogger event either of us had attended; we didn't know what was meant to happen, but for some reason I knew then that we would be seeing more of each other.

At that time, Kit was working as a stylist's assistant and I was finishing the second year of my BA in graphic design. I suspect our worlds would never have collided had it not been for a particular pair of lace tights I happened to be wearing to the event that had caught Kit's attention. I'd started sewing beads onto them the previous night, but only one leg had been completed. I started talking about customising clothes, and I soon learnt from Kit that fashion DIY was a regular part of her job on the photoshoots she assisted with.

Having graduated with qualifications for pattern cutting, Kit knew how to make a dress from scratch, while I was the wide-eyed 22-year-old living on a student budget who wanted to

learn how to make even the smallest things (like a pair of socks) from scratch. That's how I'd gotten into fashion DIY, and eventually I began sharing my projects online through my blog site. For my first project, I slashed up an ill-fitting pair of jeans and added chains to them – I cherished them as my first ALEXANDER WANGs. Kit's expertise and interest was channelled in a similar manner, although much later, which she also published on her own blog site. Her blog was mainly focused on street style in London, and included pictures of stylish people whom she had approached and photographed in the city. Her first DIY tutorial surfaced nearly two years later, in the form of a project involving a pair of bejewelled lace gloves that she had bedecked in 65 beads, 10 chains, 9 buttons and 2 earrings.

In the meantime, Kit and I were having more lattes, talking about everything and nothing, while traipsing around London and shooting material for our respective blogs. She'd wear her DIY creations that would inspire my next project, and my little projects would equally inspire her next.

And so, after nearly five years of friendship and countless collaborations, this is our first book.

We have drawn inspiration from all over the globe for the projects inside: from films, magazines and the Internet, to things we've seen on the city streets, and even from the contents of our own bedrooms. Not all of our projects can be whipped together in 20 minutes, but many of them can – and a few in even less time! Although some of them will take hours, the results are well worth it. We have tried to make sure that there is something for every style, including classic projects that we hope will continue to inspire our readers even after many years of owning this book.

The materials you'll require for the projects are inexpensive, and many of the tools you'll probably find in your (or your mother's) biscuit tin. We have divided the book into easy-to-follow chapters. Each project has simple, step-by-step instructions, supported by photographs for clearer understanding. The projects involve constructing and deconstructing, customising, embellishing and trimming fashionwear.

We hope that by using this book you will be able to breathe new life, and love, to some neglected pieces in your wardrobe. What's more, the ideas might even inspire you to pursue your own DIY adventures.

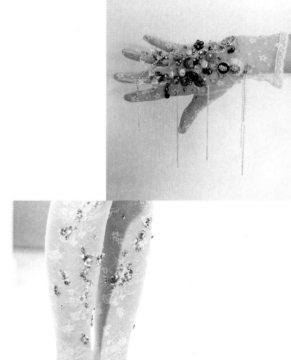

Above, right: Kit's bejewelled lace gloves. Above, left: my embellished lace tights

DIFFICULTY LEVELS EXPLAINED

1 / 5   Easy projects that do not involve sewing, and are doable while you enjoy a mug of coffee and a biscuit.

2 / 5   May include sewing, but still pretty doable while listening to music.

3 / 5   Simple machine-sewing projects.

4 / 5   More involved machine-sewing projects.

5 / 5   Pattern-making projects that may require taking notes and turning the radio off.

MATERIALS & TOOLS

Before putting your shoes on, look in your wardrobe and dig out your old clothes. Keep rooting around until you hit the back wall. You'll be surprised at how many items you find in there: broken jewellery, a skirt you grew out of, moth-eaten cardigans that can spare an arm or two. The key to a successful DIY project is being able to reinvent the fashionwear and rekindle the love you had when you first bought that item.

Now, head to the market – ask the jewellery seller whether they have a bag of broken products they'd like to get rid of, pop into the hardware store and have a poke at the bronze piping and ropes, then head to your local charity store for second-hand and vintage clothing. Raid the discount bins for any interesting fabrics and shapes.

Search online. Auction sites like eBay and Etsy are not just a source of new and second-hand clothing and haberdashery supplies, but rare ones too, such as eccentric trimmings and measuring tapes from the 1920s! They're also the perfect place to bid for a second-hand sewing machine, if you don't own one already.

INSIDE OUR BISCUIT TIN

ASSORTMENT OF THREADS made of silk, cotton or polycotton, used for hand- and machine-sewing.

BULL DOG (BINDER) CLIPS OR CLOTHES PEGS to hold glued or heavy-duty objects in place while adhesive sets.

CLOTH OR FABRIC SCRAPS to assess sewing machine stitch length, style and tensions.

CRAFT PLIERS to grab intricate objects firmly, and close up jump rings or chain rings.

CUTTER OR HEAVY-DUTY SCISSORS to cut metal, leather, plastic and art stencils.

DRESSMAKER'S PINS to hold and keep fabrics in place.

FABRIC SCISSORS to cut fabric and leather.

GLUE GUN AND MULTI-PURPOSE ADHESIVE for working on a range of arts and crafts – avoid using on fabric.

HAMMER to assist hole-punching and eyelet setting.

LIGHTER for sealing raw edges to prevent them from fraying.

MEASURING TAPE AND RULER for markings, measurements and drawing straight lines.

PAINTBRUSHES to apply paint and glue on surfaces, and brush away loose debris.

REVOLVING PUNCH PLIERS to punch holes in fabric and leather to create eyelets and belt holes.

SAFETY PINS as a suitable alternative to dressmaker's pins.

SANDPAPER AND NAIL FILE for filing and sharpening scissor blades.

SEAM RIPPER for unpicking stitches in fabric and for cutting open button holes.

SEWING MACHINE to stitch fabric and other materials together.

SEWING NEEDLES for hand-sewing fabric, beading, buttons and embroidery.

SMALL SCISSORS to snip off threads and loose trims.

TAILOR'S CHALK AND PENCIL to mark fabric temporarily for making alterations.

TWEEZERS to handle delicate materials such as gold leaf and small beads.

YARN to create pompoms.

ZIPPER FOOT to sew zips onto fabric.

KIT'S TRICKS

Five handy tips that will prepare you for any project

01 | **READ THE LABEL** Always follow the instructions on care labels to prevent damage to clothing and fabrics. This applies particularly to ironing vintage synthetic-silk scarves. If the setting is too high, the fabric will melt! Trust me. Been there, done that. Total devastation.

02 | **KNOW YOUR FABRIC** Consider the behaviour of the fabric when it is being cut, ironed or stretched. Does it curl up? Does it fray? Does it lose its shape when worn?

03 | **THROUGH THE NEEDLE'S EYE** Not everyone has the eyesight required to insert a thread through the eye of a needle. Here's a trick: snip the thread at an angle with scissors to create a pointy tip, dab a bit of moisture from your saliva on the thread, and ease it through the needle's eye.

04 | **TWIN POWER** When hand-sewing or beading, double-threaded stitching will add strength and durability to your creations.

05 | **KEEP YOUR HOUSE IN ORDER** Be organised with your beads and sequins. Use egg cups or tea-light holders to separate and store beads and sequins for your embellishment projects.

TOPS & KNITWEAR

CHAIN-STRAP CAMISOLE

The chain rule

There's nothing sexier than a slinky silk camisole, especially when the weather warms up and the days get longer. But here's another way to turn up the heat. Swap the fabric straps for ones made of chain and give the camisole an instant rock-chic look.

WHAT YOU'LL NEED

A simple strappy camisole
Fabric scissors
Lighter
1 metre (3 feet) of metal chain (it should be a similar width to the original camisole strap)
4 x jump rings
Pins
Sewing needle
Matching colour thread
Pliers

DIFFICULTY LEVEL

2/5

Use a gold-coloured chain for a more romantic look.

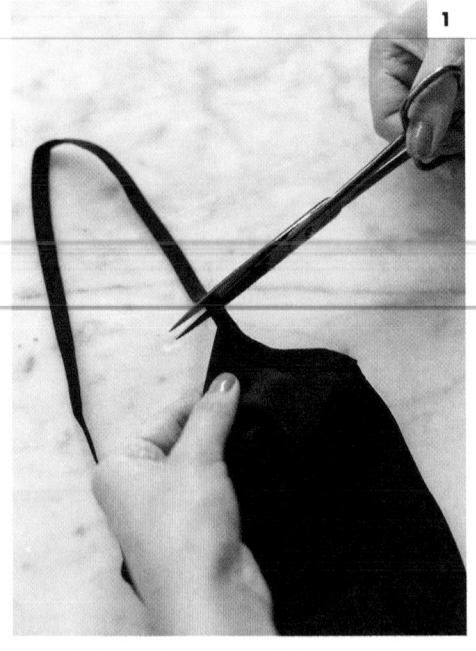

Cut both shoulder straps off, leaving short ends of about 2½ cm (1 inch) intact on both shoulders, front and back.

Light a flame close to the raw edge of the short end to seal it. This will prevent the fabric from fraying.

Use the shoulder strap as a guide to measure the chain. If the chain is too long, use pliers to shorten it.

Insert the short end to one of the straps through a jump ring.

Fold the end over to the back. Use a pin to secure, if necessary.

Hand stitch the end down to secure.

Attach the chain to the jump ring using pliers. Repeat steps 2–7 on the opposite end, and then on the front and back of the other strap. Your top is now ready to wear!

SCARF & CHAIN HALTER-NECK TOP

A French Riviera holiday

This top reminds us of a glamorous holiday by the sea or an after-dinner stroll on the boardwalk. We found this beautiful vintage silk scarf in a thrift store and transformed it into a luxurious top simply by threading in a thick chain necklace. There are about a million things you can do with a good scarf, and some of them require only a needle and thread. Check out some of our other projects involving scarves on pages 79 and 103.

DIFFICULTY LEVEL

2 / 5

WHAT YOU'LL NEED

Medium-sized silk scarf
Safety pins
Chunky chain necklace
Sewing needle
Matching colour thread

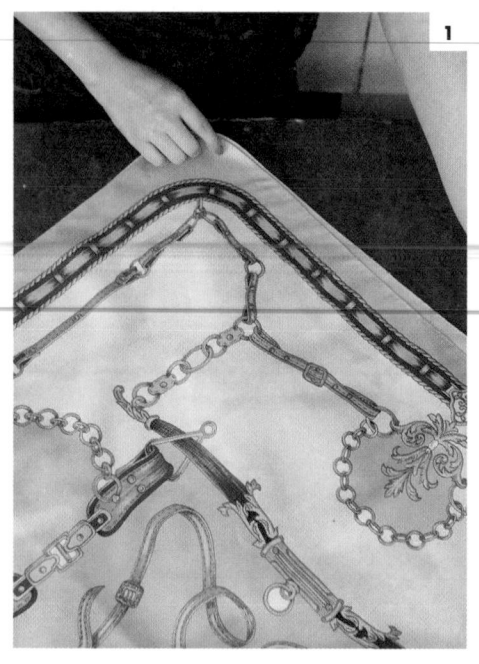

Taking opposite corners, fold the scarf in half to form a triangle.

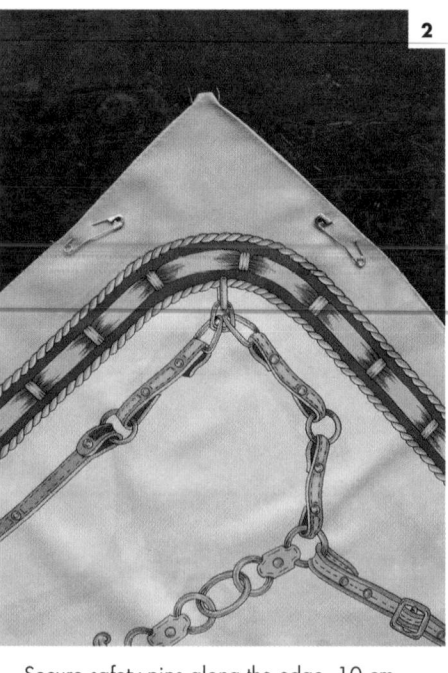

Secure safety pins along the edge, 10 cm (4 inches) away from the tip on both sides.

Place the chain necklace on top of the scarf in line with the safety pins. Fold the small corner of the scarf down.

Tuck the pointy corner in to create a straight line and secure in place with a safety pin.

To wear the scarf, put the chain necklace around your neck and tie the scarf at the back to secure.

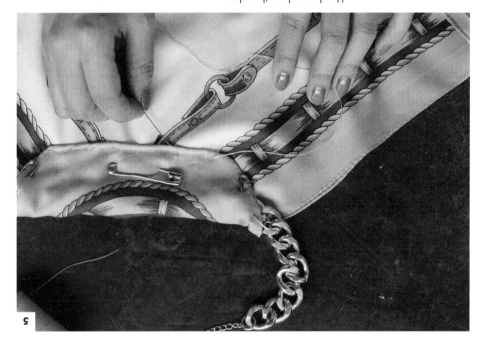

Hand-sew along the edge.

Some styling tips...

GATHERER

Ruche the neckline slightly to allow the scarf
to drape naturally.

ROLY-POLY

Roll the hem up before tying at the back for
a cropped-top effect.

LONG SHIRT *with* CROSS-OPEN ZIP

Shirt-dress and zips combo

Shirt tucked in or left outside the trousers? Let's be honest, although a classic wardrobe staple, a white shirt can be boring at times. Well, here's one idea to jazz up a long white shirt using just two zips. It's a super edgy look – literally.

You can use all kinds of zips to add contrast to the shirt. Try concealed zips for an understated look, or neon zips for a streak of colour.

WHAT YOU'LL NEED	**DIFFICULTY LEVEL**
Long white shirt	5/5
Measuring tape	
Pencil	
Ruler	
Fabric scissors	
Iron	
2 x open-ended metal teeth zips, combined measuring the length of the width of the fully-opened shirt	
Pins	
Matching colour thread	
Sewing machine with zipper foot	

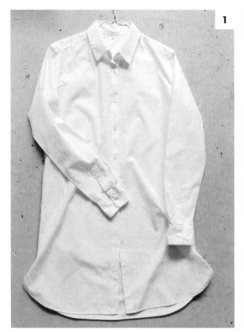

1

Lay the shirt flat on your work surface.

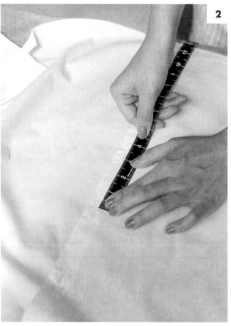

2

Determine a good length from the bottom of the shirt to place the zips – ideally just below the waist.

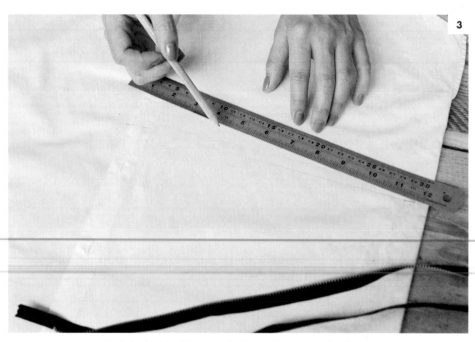

3

Mark the length with a pencil. Draw a line across the shirt using a ruler, but don't forget to add 1¼ cm (½ inch) seam allowance, above and below the line.

Extend the line across the back of the shirt.

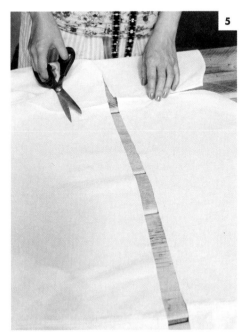

Cut along the line you have drawn. Now you have two pieces of the shirt: a top part and lower part.

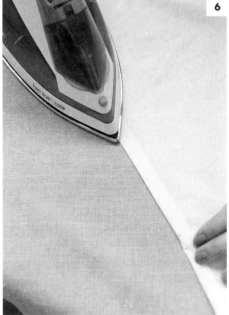

Iron the seam allowance inwards for a neater edge.

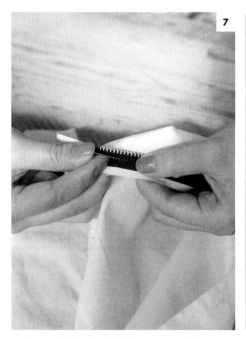

7

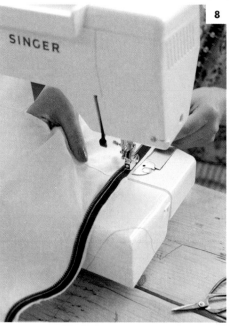

8

Open the first zip. On the top part of the shirt, place one half of the zip under the seam-fold, close to the edge. Pin to secure.

Sew a straight stitching line close to the metal teeth, removing the pins as you go.

9

Turn the shirt over and sew a straight stitching line across the back to strengthen the fastening. Repeat steps 6–9 to attach the other half of the zip to the lower part of the shirt, then repeat twice more to attach your second zip.

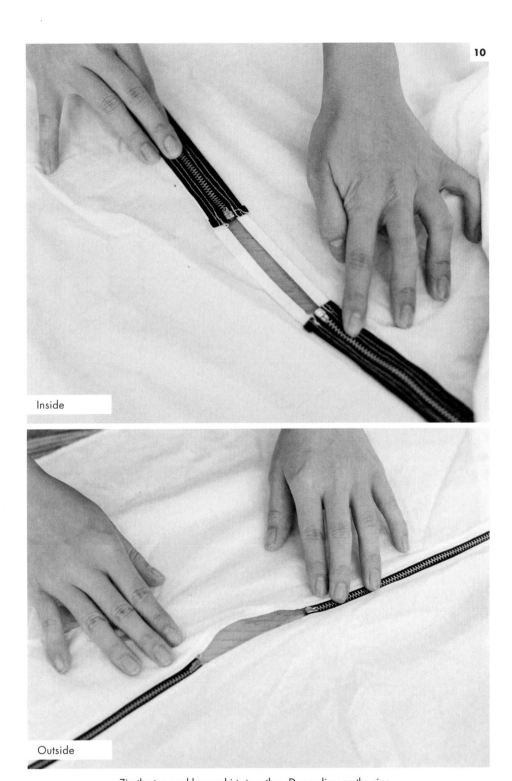

Inside

Outside

Zip the top and lower shirts together. Depending on the size of the shirt used, you may end up with a small peep-hole at the back. Press between the zips to neaten up. Wear the shirt with a simple black skirt for ultimate chic style.

POMPOM SWEATER

One thousand lightbulbs

We can't help but think of fairy lights when we look at these pompom trimmings. You must agree it's the perfect holiday sweater – move over, Santa, we're in charge of this present. Although, it's also perfect to pull on when you're lounging at home, any time of the year!

WHAT YOU'LL NEED

2 x 1 metre (3 feet) brightly coloured pompom trimmings in different colours, or home-made pompoms (see page 123)

Fabric scissors

Cable-knit sweater

Pins

Matching colour thread

Sewing needle

DIFFICULTY LEVEL

2 / 5

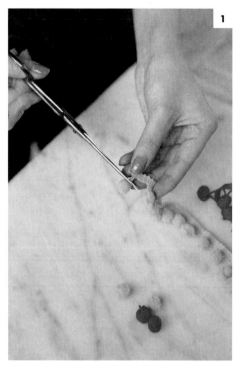

1

Detach the pompoms from the trimming with a pair of fabric scissors.

2

Lay the sweater flat on your work surface and arrange the pompoms on top in different combinations. Pin to secure.

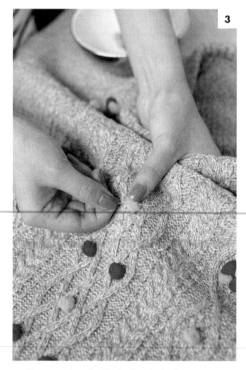

3

Once you've decided what looks best, sew the pompoms onto the sweater.

Try to be creative with your pattern. This is a fun project to brighten up the winter months – and your wardrobe!

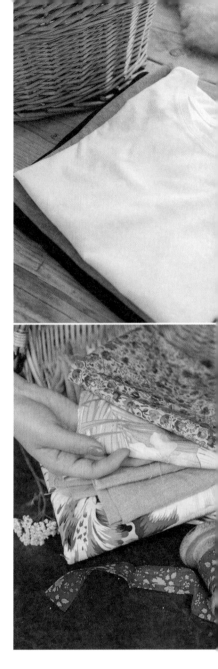

FLORAL PATCH-POCKET T-SHIRT

Adorned in nature's beauty

Even the most basic T-shirt craves some attention, and this is a super easy way to liven up any loose-fitting T-shirt you own. It'll be perfect for a warm summer's day or a stroll by the river. All you need now is some good company and a few snacks in your bag.

WHAT YOU'LL NEED

Cardboard
Ruler and pen
Fabric scissors
Liberty print fabric
Iron
Loose-fitting T-shirt
Pins
Matching coloured thread
Sewing machine

DIFFICULTY LEVEL

3 / 5

Measure and cut out a cardboard template for your pocket patch. Don't forget to include 2½ cm (1 inch) seam allowance and an extra 2½ cm (1 inch) for the top section to be folded over.

2

Cut the pocket out, using the template as a guide.

Turn the pocket wrong-side up, fold in the seam allowance then press with a hot iron, using the template to secure the fold.

Fold the top section down and press with a hot iron. Machine stitch a line across the top – this will be the opening to your pocket.

Lay the T-shirt flat on your work surface. Place the patch over the chest, preferably on the left bust, ensuring the stitched top-side is the right way up. Pin to secure.

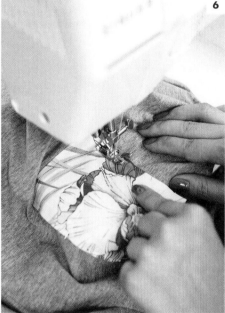

Sew on your patch pocket using a straight stitching line close to the edge, removing the pins as you go. Don't sew the top section to the T-shirt. You now have your patch pocket!

DUO-TONED CARDIGAN

A two-for-one offer

The cardigan you laze around in is all about comfort. It's cosy, casual and probably understated. This is our version, with a bit of a twist. There's nothing over the top about the two colours we've chosen, so please feel free to experiment with more contrasting colours. The best thing about this project is that it makes two, so you'll instantly have a 'his and hers'. Alternatively, give the second one as a gift to your best friend or sibling.

WHAT YOU'LL NEED

2 x fine-knitted cardigans in different colours
Iron
Measuring tape
Tailor's chalk
Fabric scissors
Pins
Matching colour thread
Sewing machine

DIFFICULTY LEVEL

4 / 5

Lay one cardigan flat on your work surface, and fold length-wise in half. Iron the crease for guidance.

On the back, on the left-side of the crease, draw a dotted line 1¼ cm (½ inch) from the fold, for seam allowance.

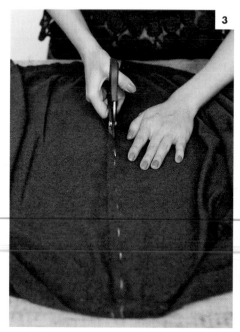

Now cut along the dotted line.

Repeat steps 1–3 with the other cardigan, but this time draw the dotted line on the right side of the creased fold.

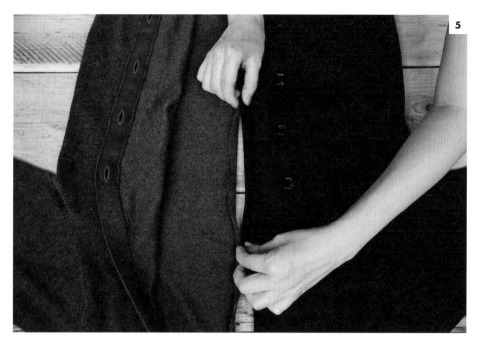

Line up the left half of one cardigan with the right half of the other. Pin together along the seam allowance to secure.

Sew a straight stitching line along the seam allowance, removing the pins as you go. Iron the seam flat to give it a nice finish. Repeat steps 5–6 with the other halves of the cardigans. You should end up with two matching duo-toned cardigans.

SKIRTS

MESH-PANEL UNDERSKIRT

Fit to flirt!

Show your sexy side with this classic, tailored skirt feauturing a mesh panel that will fool everyone at first glance. It's a great way to draw attention to your legs and express the sassy side of your personality.

WHAT YOU'LL NEED

Mesh fabric
Mini skirt
Measuring tape
Pins
Tailor's chalk
Fabric scissors
Matching colour thread
Sewing machine

DIFFICULTY LEVEL

4 / 5

First decide the width and length of the mesh underskirt, according to the size of your mini skirt. Include a 2½ cm (1 inch) seam allowance along the top and ends.

Cut out two single panel pieces using your fabric scissors. We've opted for a single panel mesh measuring 10 cm (4 inches) in length.

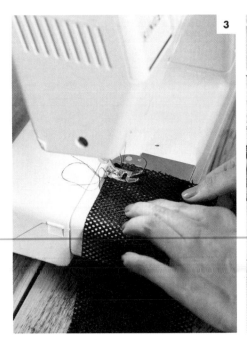

Join the ends of the mesh together and pin to secure. These will be your side seams. Sew along the seam allowance with a straight stitching line.

You should end up with a 'looped' mesh panel. Align the top of the panel under the folded hem of the mini skirt, making sure the side seams line up.

Overlap the inside hem of the skirt with your mesh panel by 5 cm (2 inches). Pin to secure.

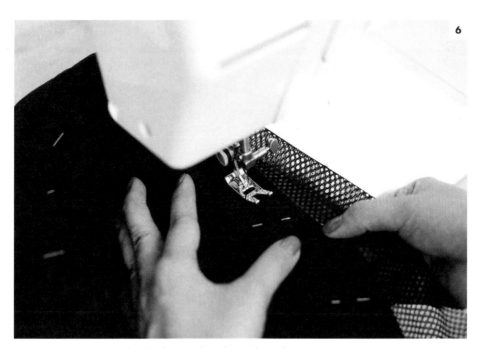

Sew the skirt hem and mesh panel together, removing the pins as you go. Cut off any loose threads.

To complete the look, dress up your skirt with an Embellished Varsity Jacket (see page 61).

Fold up $1\frac{1}{4}$ cm ($\frac{1}{2}$ inch) of the mesh at the bottom and sew for a clean edge. This will also prevent the mesh from curling up if it is stretched when worn.

FRONT-EMBELLISHED SKIRT

Where teardrops fall

This charming embellished skirt has a definite wow factor. Can you see how it will dazzle brilliantly from all angles in the light? We've used teardrop earrings for our skirt – so simple and yet so stylish. Why hasn't anyone thought of using bejewelled earrings as embellishments before?

WHAT YOU'LL NEED

Pliers

A handful of bejewelled earrings (2 x styles)

A-line mini skirt

Pins

Camera (optional)

Matching colour thread

Sewing needle

DIFFICULTY LEVEL

2 / 5

Use plastic or lightweight earrings for this project, and make sure the skirt is made of thick woven fabric (boucle or leather would be ideal). Avoid using heavy, metal earrings; you don't want to add weight to the skirt, plus the hard edges might even tear the fabric.

Start by removing all fasteners behind the earrings (butterflies, posts, hinges, clips and hooks). Use pliers to help you, as this can be a bit tricky.

Lay the skirt flat on your work surface. Think about where you'd like to place the bejewelled pieces.

Insert pins to mark the earring positions, or take a photo to remember the pattern.

Using a needle and thread, find a gap, hole or hoop in the earrings to sew to the skirt.

Once you've attached all the earrings on, your newly bejewelled skirt is ready to wear.

COATS & JACKETS

EMBELLISHED VARSITY JACKET

Sporty and star-studded

What can a bold appliqué do to enhance the look of a sports jacket? The answer is, lots! By sewing on interesting patterns or decorating the jacket with delightful little beads, gems and jewellery, you'll make a fashion statement that'll put you in a different league altogether!

WHAT YOU'LL NEED

Varsity jacket

Assortment of beads, buttons, broken jewellery and gemstones

Tailor's chalk

Camera (optional)

Matching colour thread

Sewing needle

DIFFICULTY LEVEL

2 / 5

Use small, kitschy iron-on appliqué patterns for extra decoration.

Lay the jacket flat on your work surface.

Place the adornments anywhere on the jacket, then stand back to see how it looks.

Mark the positioning with chalk, or take a photo to remember the pattern. Sew the adornments to the fabric, but be careful not to sew through any pockets.

Once complete, try it on in front of the mirror and marvel at your masterpiece!

Go wild with your embellishing – sew on as much as you can!

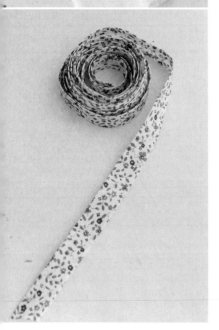

RAINCOAT with FLORAL PRINT TRIMS

Shine on a rainy day

Add a touch of cuteness and femininity to your dull see-through raincoat with decorative trims. Perfect for a little fun and romance in the drizzle. New York, London, Paris, here we come!

WHAT YOU'LL NEED

4 metres (13 feet) of floral print, single fold bias tape (enough to cover front opening, sleeve cuffs, hood and hem)
Measuring tape
Fabric scissors
Raincoat
Pins
Matching colour thread
Sewing machine

DIFFICULTY LEVEL

4 / 5

Open out one side of the bias fold. With the floral-print side down, line it up to the inside edge of the raincoat. Pin to secure it.

Measure the amount of bias tape you need for each area.

Sew along the bias fold with a straight stitching line.

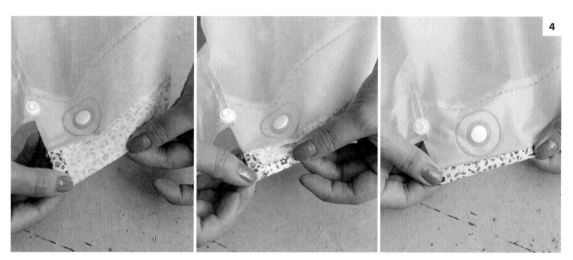

Turn the raincoat right side up and open out the bias tape. Fold the bias tape fully around the edge of the raincoat. The sides of the bias tape should line up on the inside and outside edges of the raincoat. Pin to secure.

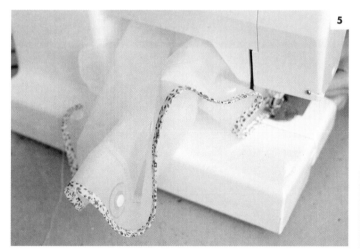

Sew a straight stitching line close to the outside edge of the bias tape, removing the pins as you go.

Repeat steps 1–5 to decorate the other parts of the raincoat.

Now you're ready to greet the rain in style!

BOUCLÉ JACKET with GOLD CHAIN TRIM

A chain reaction

This old jacket may have been languishing in your wardrobe, but our gold chain detail will add a sleek and compelling dimension to the textured bouclé fabric and colour, giving the jacket a modern look. Perfect for the boardroom or a night out in town.

WHAT YOU'LL NEED

Bouclé jacket
Gold chain
Pliers
Matching colour thread
Sewing needle

DIFFICULTY LEVEL

2 / 5

Lay the jacket on your work surface. Place the chain close to the edge of the zip and around the collar, then down the other side of the zip. Gauge the length you'll need.

Use pliers to seperate the chain into three sections: a section for the front of the jacket, and a section each for the two sleeve cuffs.

Using a needle and thread, run a looping stitch from under the fabric. Sew every second or third link, depending on the thickness and weight of the chain.

Repeat step 3 to attach the chain to both sleeve cuffs. Cut off any loose threads to neaten the finish. This is a great way to breathe life into an unused jacket.

Some tips...

Avoid using fabric scissors to cut the chain, as the metal will damage the scissor blades.

Use pins to secure the chain on the fabric to stop it from moving around while hand-stitching.

DRESSES

FRONT ASYMMETRICAL TIERED FRINGE DRESS

Happy, flappy and carefree

We love a long fringe cascading on a dress, giving it a sleek and flirty feel. Perfect for dancing the Charleston, or perhaps for strutting down the street in high stilettos and letting the fringe do its own dance.

WHAT YOU'LL NEED

Fitted dress

2 metres (6½ feet) of 28 cm (11 inch) looped chainette fringe trim, or cut-end fringe trim

Fabric scissors

Pins

Lighter (optional)

Matching colour thread

Sewing machine

DIFFICULTY LEVEL

4 / 5

Lay the dress flat on your work surface. Decide what angle you'd like the fringe tilted on the dress, and the number of tiers you want.

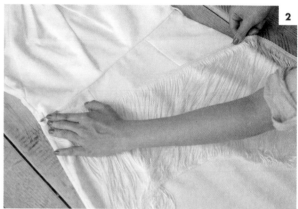

To create the first tier, lay out the fringe at your chosen angle on the dress. Cut the end and remember to leave 1 ¼ cm (½ inch) on each side. If you are using looped fringe, do not snip the loops. Pin to secure.

To create the second tier, lay out the fringe so that the fringing from the first tier overlaps the second by about 5 cm (2 inches). Cut, then pin to secure. Repeat the same method for any subsequent tiers.

The braided top that holds looped fringe tends to unravel. To prevent this (if you are using looped fringe), light a flame close to each edge and let it melt. It will harden to cool.

Set the sewing machine to the zig-zag stitch setting. Fold in the side edges, and run the zig-zag stitch along the fringe's braided top. Repeat this step on the other tiers, removing the pins as you go.

If using looped fringe, snip the loops.

Put the dress on a hanger, let the fringe cascade, and stand back and admire.

KAFTAN SCARF DRESS

"Buongiorno signora!"

Add a touch of Sicilian class to your scarf-print kaftan dress and emulate the romantic summers, giddy opulence and baroque style of the region. *Ciao bella!*

WHAT YOU'LL NEED

2 x medium-sized print scarves (square shaped)

Measuring tape

Mannequin (optional)

Pins

Matching colour thread

Sewing machine

DIFFICULTY LEVEL

3 / 5

Use rectangle-shaped scarves to create a full-length kaftan dress.

To create the front section of the dress, take
your first scarf and fold it in half, lengthways.

Firmly crease the fold mark at the top and place a
pin in the crease. This is your mark for the centre-
front. Use it as a reference point.

To create a shoulder point, measure your desired width from either side of the centre-front. For guidence, hold it up to your body or use a mannequin, lining the centre-front with the middle of your neck. Pin to secure.

Line up the other scarf and put the pins in the same places. Pin the two scarves together where the shoulder points should be. Leave the seam open from the shoulder to create a split opening for each sleeve.

Turn the garment inside out, making sure the pins stay in place. Sew a straight stitching-line along the edge to close up the shoulder points, leaving 2½ cm (1 inch) seam allowance. Careful you don't sew the arms or neckline. Do the same for the side seams.

Use your measuring tape to determine the length of the arm openings. Place a pin where you want the side seams to start.

Carefully remove all the pins, turn the garment back the right way, and drape over your body to check it fits correctly. *Finito!*

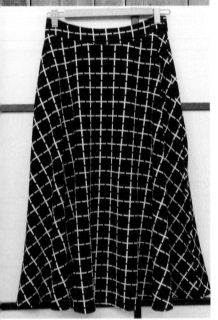

T-SHIRT & SKIRT FROCK

Frill-seeker

The peplum trend has come and gone, but the frilly skirt is here to stay. What's more, it can be part of a dress! By combining the two garments, we've created a super daring T-shirt and skirt frock. We call it, grunge-gone-cute.

WHAT YOU'LL NEED

Oversized T-shirt
A-line skirt
Measuring tape or ruler
Tailor's chalk
Fabric scissors
Pins
Matching colour thread
Sewing machine
Iron

DIFFICULTY LEVEL

5 / 5

Lay the T-shirt on your work surface. If you need to shorten it, cut the bottom hem off up to the hip level. You want to create a drop-waist dress.

Lay the A-line skirt on your work surface. At the bottom hem, measure the length you want for the skirt section. Mark with chalk, making sure you add 2½ cm (1 inch) for seam allowance.

Mark the same length across the whole width of the skirt, then cut along the line to remove the bottom part. Discard the top part of the skirt, or save it for a new project.

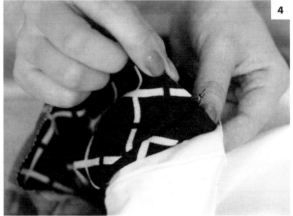

Pin the bottom seam of the T-shirt to the top seam of the skirt. You will see, as you go along, how much skirt fabric you will need to gather and pleat.

Make sure the pleated skirt is the same width as the bottom of the T-shirt, and that they are securely pinned together.

Try to gather the skirt fabric into even pleats. Pin as you go along, to secure them in place.

Sew a straight stitching line along the seam allowance, ensuring the pleats stay in place. Remove the pins as you go.

Once complete, straighten out your pleats and iron the seam flat to give the skirt a nice finish.

ACCESSORIES & BAGS

EMBELLISHED SLOUCHY SOCKS

Snowflakes on my toes

Spice up your woolly socks with extra sparkles using unworn or broken bits of jewellery. Wear them slouched just above the ankles, and style them with a pair of killer heels for a drool-worthy investment that will look awesome, while keeping your toes lovely and cosy.

WHAT YOU'LL NEED

Diamanté jewellery
Pliers
Thick pair of ribbed woollen socks
Matching colour thread
Sewing needle

DIFFICULTY LEVEL

1 / 5

Carefully remove the diamanté studs from the jewellery, using pliers.

Divide the diamanté studs into equal amounts for each sock.

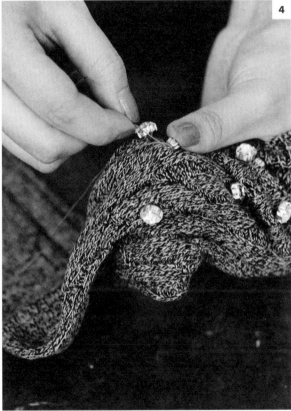

Place the studs anywhere you like, but do not overload.

Mark the positioning of the studs with pins. Sew them on with the needle and thread.

Wear with a pair of chunky wedge heels to really show these gems off.

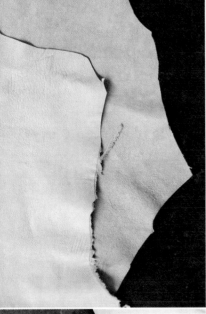

SLOUCHY LEATHER LUNCH BAG

The sumptuous food pouch

Drawing inspiration from the classic brown paper bag, famous for stowing take-out food and groceries, we've created our own version in soft white Napa leather.

WHAT YOU'LL NEED

Soft leather (Napa)
Ruler
Pencil
Fabric scissors
Pins
Matching colour thread
Sewing machine
Cardboard

DIFFICULTY LEVEL

4 / 5

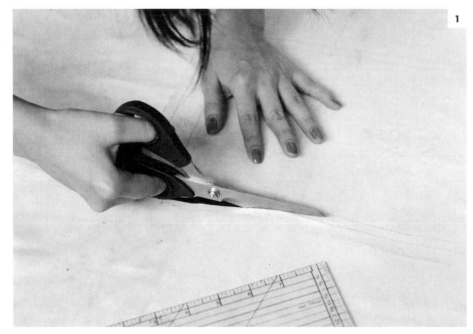

Lay the leather sheet on your work surface with the polished side facing down, and decide the ideal size and depth of your lunch bag. Measure and draw two rectangle side panels, a front panel, back panel and a base panel (five pieces in total). Don't forget to add 2½ cm (1 inch) seam allowance around each piece and 5 cm (2 inches) to the top section to be folded over.

Cut out the panels. (The base panel is not featured in the picture.)

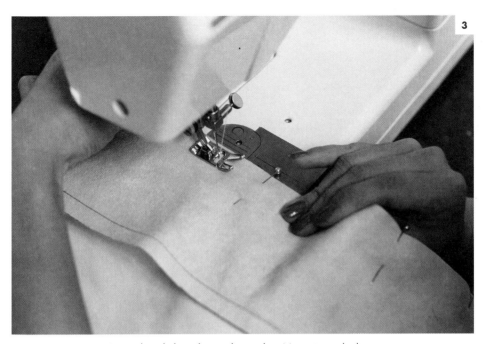

Pin and stitch the side panels together. Now pin on the base to line up correctly in the corners. Trim the corners to avoid any bulky fabric. Carefully stitch the base on. The bag should be inside out.

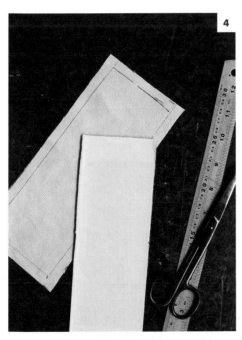

Cut out a piece of cardboard the size of the base panel, to use for support.

Push the bag the right way out, and insert the cardboard to line the base of the bag.

To finish, fasten the bag with a stylish, thin black belt (see page 101).

Some tips...

Use a leather machine needle in the sewing
machine for easy stitching.

Use a lubricant such as petroleum jelly
(Vaseline) or silicone spray to prevent
friction between the leather and the sewing
machine.

SCARF-WRAPPED PURSE STRAP

Weave a bit of magic

It's a new bag! Or is it? Next time you're on holiday and wanting to have fun accessorising, grab a colourful scarf and you're ready to revitalise a bag. A simple alteration to the strap will make it look like something you bought on holiday as a souvenir.

WHAT YOU'LL NEED

Large silk printed scarf
Small shoulder bag with strap and metal D-rings or eyelets

DIFFICULTY LEVEL

1 / 5

Insert the scarf through the eyelet or D-ring, and tie the end into a small knot.

Twist and weave the scarf around the bag strap.

Insert the end of the scarf through the eyelet or D-ring, and tie it into a small knot to finish.

Update a vintage bag with this trick!

PAINTED ACRYLIC CLUTCH BAG

Zig-ah-zig-AH

In keeping with the art deco influence while adding our own contemporary twist, we've decorated a neon acrylic clutch bag with a striking geometric design that would glam up any outfit. Make it your own and no one else's.

WHAT YOU'LL NEED

Neon transparent acrylic clutch bag

Masking tape

Scissors

2 x paint brushes

Black and white acrylic paints

Scrap paper

DIFFICULTY LEVEL

2 / 5

Before you start, make sure the clutch bag is clean. Remove all dirt and oil stains with a clean cloth. Take off any additional detailing, such as straps or inner pouches.

Create the first row of a zig-zag pattern on the front of the clutch bag using masking tape. Repeat the same pattern on the back and sides.

Cover your work surface with scrap paper. Begin painting the unmasked area in acrylic paint, alternating in shades of black and white. Repeat the pattern on the sides.

Leave the paint to dry, then paint the back of the clutch. When dry, apply a second layer of paint to the front and sides. Leave to dry before painting a second layer on the back.

Once the paint is fully dry, carefully remove the masking tape.

Reattach the straps and inner pouch, if required. Your clutch bag is ready!

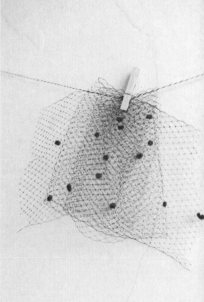

VEIL & POMPOM RIBBON-TOP CAP

Fuzzy feeling

When the warm weather arrives, there's nothing quite like stepping outside wearing a personalised summer cap adorned in a spotted veil and fluffy pompoms. You'll be sporting something that looks a little bit like bunny ears, but it's certain to get the whole world smiling at you.

WHAT YOU'LL NEED

Spotted veiling
Fabric scissors
Patterned cap
Sewing needle
Matching colour thread
Pompoms (see page 123 if you want to make your own)

DIFFICULTY LEVEL

1 / 5

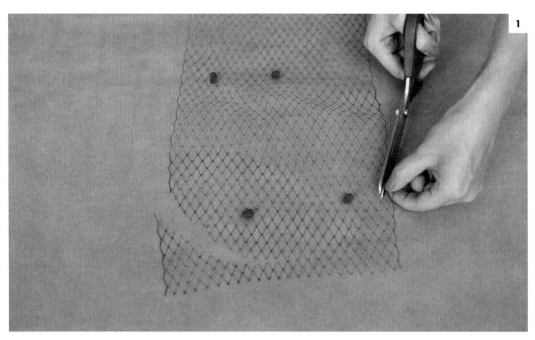

Take a small rectangular piece of spotted veiling, and cut the corners to round them off.

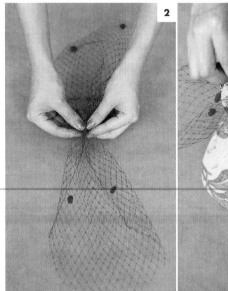

Tie the veil into a bow, but don't make the knot too tight!

Place the bow centrally on the front of the cap and sew in place.

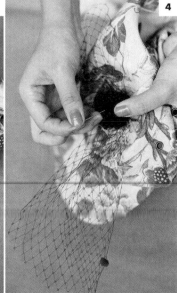

Place the pompoms over the bow's knot. Sew securely in place.

Your cute veil and pompom cap is ready to wear.

Some tips...

You can accessorise a simple head-band in the same way: simply tie the bow around the band and sew on the pompoms!

Experiment with the decorations. Glue or sew a bejewelled animal or insect brooch onto the pompom, for an added fun factor.

COTTON WASH BAG

Jungle survival kit

At times it feels like we live out of our suitcases, so naturally we like to pack our wash bags with as much as possible – skincare products, ladies' grooming tools, a manicure kit. In this instance, both style and size matter! So, here's an idea we've come up with that transforms a cotton pillowcase into a bumper-size wash bag.

WHAT YOU'LL NEED

Printed pillowcase
Measuring tape
Fabric scissors
20 cm (8 inch) metallic zip
Pins
Matching colour thread
Sewing machine with zipper foot
Iron

DIFFICULTY LEVEL

4 / 5

Cut and open apart the pillow case. Measure two square panels (front and back), 20 cm x 20 cm (8 inches x 8 inches). Don't forget to include a 2½ cm (1 inch) seam allowance around the two pieces.

Cut out the two pieces. They should be identical in size.
Unzip the zip.

3

Lay down one of the panels with the right side up. Place one of the zips close to the edge with the metal teeth facing inwards. Pin to secure.

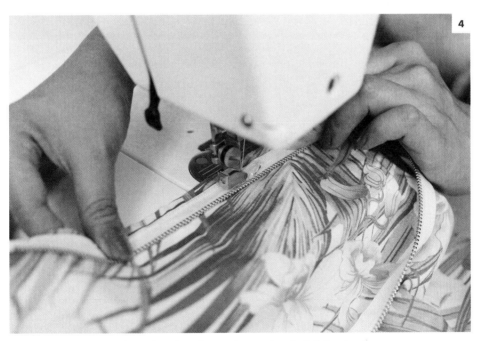

4

Sew a straight stitching line close to the metal teeth. Pull the zip along as you complete the stitching, removing the pins as you go.

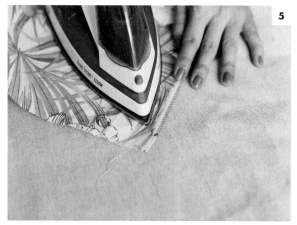

5

Give the fabric a quick press with an iron to make a neat fold around the zip.

6

Repeat steps 3–5 on the other panel and join up the zip.

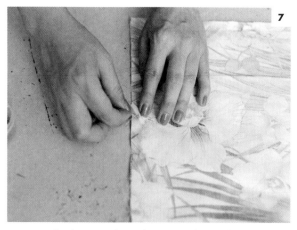

7

Flip the zipped panels wrong side round. Join the front and back panels together, ensuring they meet at the corners and are lined up correctly. Pin to secure.

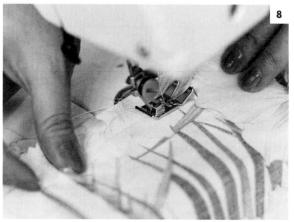

8

Remove the zipper foot from the machine. Sew a straight stitching line around the edges, removing the pins as you go.

9

Trim off any excess fabric at the zip corners to ensure you have no bulk when you turn the pouch the right way out.

Light a flame close to the raw edges to ensure they are fray-free.

You can apply binding to seal the raw seams and zip area.

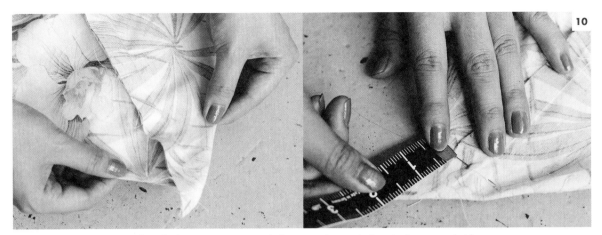

To box the bottom corners, pinch them together and align the bottom and side seams. Measure 4 cm (1½ inches) in from the point.

Mark a line with pins, then sew along the line. This is to add depth to the pouch.

Turn the pouch the right way out, and tidy along the seams.

As you can see, the boxed corners have given the bag enough depth to fit your essentials. Your wash bag is ready to use.

SHOES

POMPOM HEELS

Gimme a D! Gimme an I! Gimme a Y!

We think pompoms are the most cheerful adornments, whether they're bouncing on the top of a knitted hat during colder days, or adorning a cable-knit sweater (page 34). For this project, we've decided to attach them to our favourite pair of stiletto heels. The look is somewhat festive, but we think it can be worn with a colourful dress at any time of the year. Beware: once you start making these pompoms, you'll be hooked!

WHAT YOU'LL NEED

Two colours of knitting yarn
Fabric scissors
Pen or tweezers
Revolving punch pliers or an awl
Yarn needle
Your favourite high heels

DIFFICULTY LEVEL

3 / 5

Try picking a yarn ball that is plush to touch – the denser the yarn, the plumper the pompom. Four-ply (fingering weight yarn) is ideal for making plump pompoms.

The more times the yarn is wrapped, the fluffier and fuller your pompom will be.

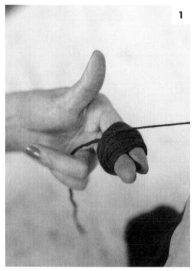

1

Leaving an 8 cm (3 inch) tail, wind the yarn around your index and middle finger about 100 times.

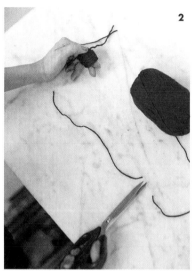

2

Snip with your scissors and cut an extra 30 cm (12 inches) of the yarn.

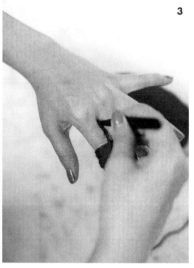

3

Squeeze the end of the yarn tail through the gap between your two fingers. To help you, push through with a pen or a pair of tweezers.

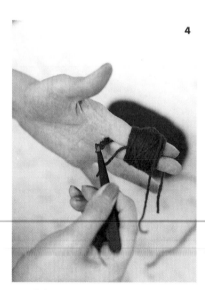

4

Pull the yarn tail out from under your fingers...

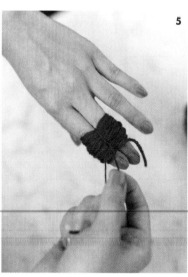

5

...and tie a strong knot on top.

6

Carefully wriggle the yarn off your fingers.

Turn over, and tie a tight double knot using the extra length of yarn.

With a sharp pair of scissors, snip the loops all the way round.

Trim down the yarn into a neat ball.

Repeat steps 1–9 to create three more pompoms. You should end up with four in total: two for each shoe in alternate colours.

Punch a hole in each shoe near the ankle.

Thread the tail of the pompoms into a yarn needle, and insert through the punched hole.

Tie a tight double knot inside. Repeat steps 11–12 with the other shoe.

These heels are the perfect way to brighten up any outfit.

DIP-PAINT BROGUES

Indulge your shoe fetish

We love a quirky pair of brogues that compete for attention with the rest of the outfit, especially the socks! A lick of brightly coloured paint on the shoes will give them a funky look. Which lucky socks will get to pop into these?

WHAT YOU'LL NEED

Brogues

Masking tape

Scrap paper

Household matt paint or permanent acrylic paint (choose a colour you like)

Paintbrush

DIFFICULTY LEVEL

2 / 5

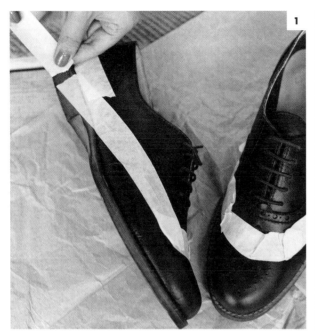

Clean your shoes before you start. Cover your work surface with scrap paper. Decide the parts you want to paint and line the rest with masking tape. Make sure the tape is firmly pressed down to prevent paintwork bleeding into the masked area.

Apply the paint on the designated area with a soft paintbrush. Add a second coat, if necessary.

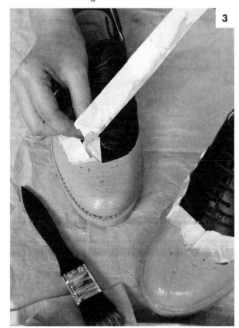

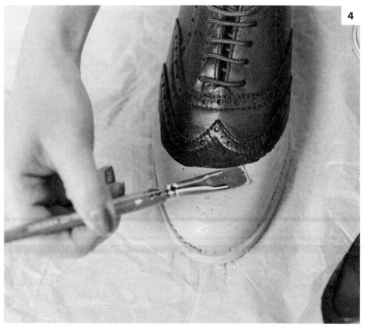

Once the paint is touch dry (it doesn't need to be completely dry), carefully peel off the masking tape, making sure the lines stay clean.

If the paintwork looks uneven, apply a touch-up. Repeat steps 2–4 on the other shoe.

Leave the shoes to dry for a whole day
before wearing.

FLOPPY BOW SHOES

A curtsy and a bow

Please your inner girl – step out in style and show off your feminine side with this cute and fanciful pair of bow-back heels. You might wish to complement the look by showing off your flirty and giggly personality. The choice is yours.

Experiment with different fabrics to create the bows (satin, velvet, organza or grosgrain).

WHAT YOU'LL NEED

A piece of small Liberty print fabric
Ruler
Pen
Fabric scissors
Pins
Matching colour thread
Sewing needle
Safety pins
Shoes with loop on the back
or a detachable strap

DIFFICULTY LEVEL

2 / 5

No need to add seam allowance. We like the edges raw.

Lay out the fabric on your work surface and draw a rectangular piece measuring 6 cm x 15 cm (2½ inches x 6 inches). You'll need four of these pieces for two bows (front and back), to add strength. Keep the edges raw.

Cut out two of the retangular pieces and pin together to secure. Hand-sew a straight stitching line close to the edges. Cut out the remaining two rectangular pieces and sew together.

Make sure the shoe has a loop on the back where the strap is inserted. Fix a safety pin in one corner of the ribbon and use it to feed the ribbon through the loop.

Pull the end until the bow is positioned centrally. Straighten and neaten the bow. Repeat steps 3–4 on other shoe. Your bows are done!

METAL CHAIN-FRINGE HEELS

Curtain call

We all crave sultry footwear that's fit for any occasion. This shimmering chain-fringe adds salsa and spice to your heels. Time to go dancing, we think!

WHAT YOU'LL NEED

About 3 metres (10 feet) of small lightweight chain

Strappy heels or shoes with straps

Measuring tape

Pliers

Safety pins

Glue gun

Scrap paper

Bull dog clips or clothes pegs

DIFFICULTY LEVEL

4 / 5

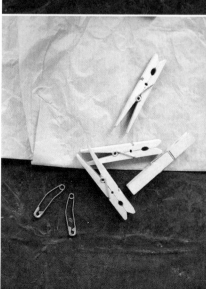

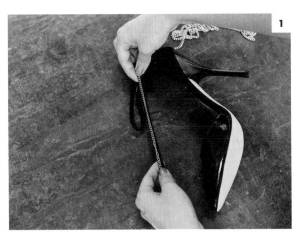

1

Measure the front strap of the shoe using a measuring tape to determine the length of your main chain strap. Use pliers to pull the chain apart and extract the main chain strap.

2

Work out how many chain fringes you'll need to attach to the loops of the main chain strap. Carefully extract your fringes from the chain.

3

Insert safety pins in each end to support the weight and prevent the chain fringe from twisting when holding the strap. Open the end loop of each chain fringe and attach to the main chain strap. Make sure the loops are securely closed up.

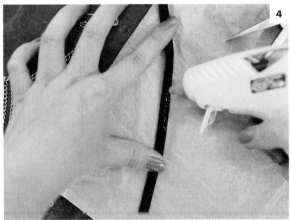

4

Heat up your glue gun. Place the shoe strap on your work surface covered with scrap paper. Apply the hot glue along the strap.

Be extra careful when using the hot glue gun. It's easy to burn yourself. Always handle with care and follow the instructions on the packet or manual.

5

Carefully place the main chain strap on the shoe strap, using a bull dog clip or clothes pegs to hold the chain and strap in place. Apply more hot glue, if necessary.

6

Leave the strap to dry and the glue to set. Repeat steps 1–6 for the other shoe.

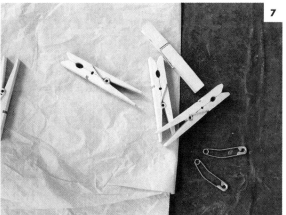

7

Remove clips and safety pins once the glue is dry, then try on your shoes and witness the instant transformation from ordinary to extraordinary.

GOLD LEAF HEELS

Picked from a golden tree

Add a touch of sophistication to your look by emblazoning your heels in gold leaf. Jazz it up with a flowing chiffon dress and dance the night away! It's a style to suit any occasion.

To save time, use metallic spray paint instead of gold leaf.

WHAT YOU'LL NEED

White stiletto heels
Clean cloth
Scrap paper
Masking tape
2 x soft paintbrushes
Water-based acrylic gold size (adhesive)
Loose gold leaf (25 sheets, 14 cm x 14 cm) (5½ inches x 5½ inches)
Tweezers
Clear Shellac varnish (sealer)

DIFFICULTY LEVEL

3 / 5

1

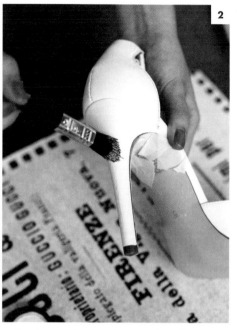

2

Firstly, wipe your shoe with a cloth until they are clean. Cover your work surface with scrap paper. Cover the strap, side panels and inside of the heels with masking tape.

Dip the paintbrush in the water-based acrylic gold size, and apply a coat to the entire heel and back panel.

3

4

Leave to dry for 15 minutes.

Gold leaf is extremely delicate and can easily crumble, so handle with care.

Once the milky adhesive is completely clear and sticky, pick up a sheet of gold leaf with tweezers and gently place it over the heel and back panel.

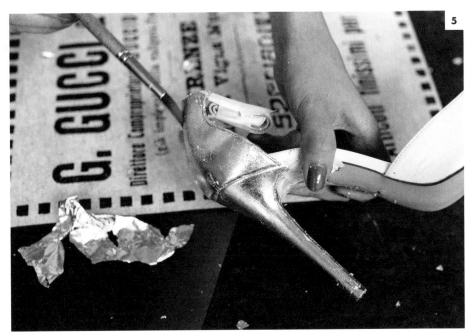

Pat and smooth it down gently on the sticky surface with a clean, soft brush. Continue to cover the area, filling in any gaps, if necessary. Smooth out creases and brush away any debris. Repeat steps 1–5 for the other shoe.

Seal the surfaces with a coat of clear Shellac sealer. Leave to dry for 15 minutes, then stand back and marvel at the golden-heeled beauties.

QUICK & EASY

Ten simple projects

01

Don't discard broken jewellery; keep and reuse to create another piece of jewellery.

02

Add 'zing' to your outfit by personalising your shirt-collar tips with bejewelled clip-on earrings – it's the perfect styling trick when you're short of time!

03

Bored of your leather pencil skirt? Cut simple geometric patterns out of hard cardboard, and use them as stencils to spray light coats of silver or gold metallic paints to give your skirt a futuristic-luxe look.

04

Jazz up your cardigan by swapping the existing buttons with bejewelled or mother-of-pearl buttons.

05

To give your leather jacket a classic old-weathered look, distress the leather by simply rubbing the surface with fine-grain sandpaper.

06

Wax your old pair of skinny jeans with a heavy-duty fabric wax, to give them the lustre look.

07

To brighten up your trainers (sneakers), swap the shoelaces for floral-print ribbons or bright neon laces.

08

Use nuts and washers as alternatives to beads for jewellery making, such as a bracelet. Apply fine coats of neon nail varnish to the surface to add colour and edge.

09

Transform your wide-legged trousers to culottes by cutting them below the knee.

10

Attach fancy corsage hair clips to your favourite pair of heels to create an instant mood change.

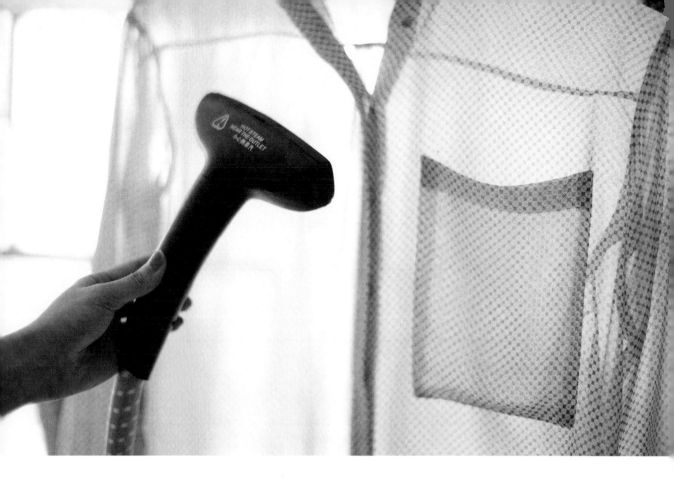

CARE AFFAIR

Eight ways to look after your masterpieces

Don't be left heartbroken by failing to take proper care of your creation or by storing it badly. You may have married two very unlikely materials, like brass piping and a silk dress, which means you'll need to think about how to look after the combination. What's more, it's easy to damage delicate materials during the making process itself. Here are some tips to help you on your way.

01 | Sewing on a button or bead sounds like an easy task for a beginner, but be aware that if sewn carelessly, threads will tend to unravel. To prevent this from occurring, apply a fine coat of clear nail polish onto the threads or knots after stitching.

02 | When working on delicate fabrics such as silk, chiffon or lace, cover the surface with tissue paper to prevent it from staining and fraying. Store projects made of delicate fabrics by wrapping them in thin tissue paper.

03 | Think about how you will clean or wash your embellished garments. For example, always hand wash embellished woollen socks (see page 90) gently with cold water and shampoo to help them retain their soft texture, then pat dry with a towel.

04 | Hot water can occasionally cause sequins and colour-coated gems to melt or lose their colour. It's advisable to hand wash such garments inside out, using the method described in tip 3.

05 | Studs and chains may rust when washed, so adorn them on items of clothing that don't need to be washed frequently, such as denim jackets, leather boots and bags. For the projects that include metallic decorations, an occasional wipe down with a dry cloth will prevent moisture gathering on the metal.

06 | Store projects involving fringe trimming, such as the white fringing dress on page 74, inside a garment bag to prevent discolouration.

07 | Acrylic paint may peel off, especially when it comes in contact with water. When painting on fabric, try using fabric paint instead and then seal with a hot iron. Use acrylic paint on items that will not need washing, such as shoes and bags.

08 | To create a ripped denim effect, cut a few short lines above the knee, and pop your jeans in a washing machine. Let them fray naturally in a normal washing cycle.

SUPPLIERS & RESOURCES

TRIMMINGS & FABRICS

UK

JOHN LEWIS

www.johnlewis.com

A great place for basic materials and tools, you will find a good range of coloured threads, knitting yarns, fashion and soft furnishing trimmings, tools, craft kits for adults and children, patterns and an excellent range of sewing machines and embroidery machines.

LIBERTY

www.liberty.co.uk

A world-famous department store with a rich heritage, best known for their iconic Liberty print fabrics and exclusive collaborations with brands such as Nike, Dr. Martens, Lavenham, Barbour, Marc by Marc Jacobs, Kenzo, Fred Perry and many more. The haberdashery department has a beautiful selection of Liberty print fabrics, knitting yarns, trimmings buttons, tools, craft books and magazines. The store also offers knitting and craft workshops.

BARNETT LAWSON TRIMMINGS

www.bltrimmings.com

A wholesale shop located in the basement of an office building. It stocks almost every trimming you can find, including boxes upon boxes of appliqué fabrics, boas, chains, D-rings, fringings, pom poms, faux flowers, ribbons and much more. They also stock millinery supplies.

KLEINS

www.kleins.co.uk

The best haberdashery for the most varied and comprehensive range of trimmings, chains, frames, fasteners, zips, ribbons, appliqué patches and dyes.

CLOTH HOUSE

www.clothhouse.com

They have unusual fabrics and an extensive range of organic fabrics, including cotton, linen and hemp. They also stock a limited range of buttons and trimmings. Popular with fashion students and up-and-coming designers.

TEMPTATION ALLEY

www.temptationalley.com

Located in trendy Notting Hill, and known as the Aladdin's cave of trimmings, this small store stocks some 15,000 (rare) products. From beaded braids, jewelled fringes and feathered braids, to fine embroidered jacquard trims. Specialises in supplying the film and TV industry, interior designers and the antiques trade.

US

MICHAELS
www.michaels.com
One of the largest retail chains across the US and Canada. Specialises in arts, crafts, framing, floral accessories, wall décor, beads, knitting, bakeware and much more. Michaels offers an exciting array of creative classes, such as cake decorating, jewellery making, paper crafting, knitting and crochet.

M&J TRIMMING
www.mjtrim.com
Located in New York City, M&J Trimming houses a wide variety of high-quality trimmings imported from around the world, including ribbons from France, laces from Switzerland, Austrian Swarovski crystals and much more.

Australia

LINCRAFT
www.lincraft.com.au
A craft store established in 2005, that sells cut-price fabric and patterns, trimmings, knitting yarns, sewing and knitting equipment, sewing machines and overlockers, curtains and blinds, basic craft supplies and homeware.

THE FABRIC STORE
www.thefabricstore.com.au
Stocks designer dress fabrics and New Zealand Merino products specialises in organic natural fibres and offers a great selection of good-quality basics such as silk, chiffon, georgette, woollen suiting, cotton, linen, leather hide and much more. Also offers a range of specialised books and patterns.

HOUSE OF ADORN
www.houseofadorn.com
Formerly known as The Feather Shop, House of Adorn stocks an array of fine feathers, fabrics and trimmings. Other products include embellishments, millinery supplies, ribbons, fabric flowers, veils, lace, essential tools and equipments, and much more.

Online

ETSY
www.etsy.com
An online marketplace for vintage and custom-made trimmings, buttons, fabrics and patterns.

EBAY
www.ebay.com
The world's largest online marketplace for almost everything, and the best place to find job lots, out of seasoned trimmings and tools at cheap price.

WANDER AND HUNT
wanderandhunt.com
Founded by DIY genius and personal friend Geneva (author of *A Pair and A Spare* blog), Wander and Hunt sells popular on-trend project kits ranging from DIY transparent satchel kits to DIY jewellery kits, as well as essential tools and other necessities.

SUPPLIERS & RESOURCES

RESOURCES

We are always on the lookout for sources of inspiration, from catwalks, street styles, music videos, editorials and past DIY projects to online material such as advertisements, webzines and blogs. Here's a list of resources that have inspired our projects.

Fashion & DIY blogs

A PAIR AND A SPARE
www.apairandasparediy.com
Geneva's endless DIY projects and moodboard inspirations, published weekly, always leave us hungry for more.

HONESTLY WTF
www.honestlywtf.com
Erica and Lauren's curated cool-hunting images, which are sourced from street-style blogs, catwalks and editorials, turn inspirational ideas into DIY projects.

LOVE AESTHETICS
www.love-aesthetics.blogspot.com
Ivania never fails to impress us with her consistent style and impressive list of inventive projects.

Online sources of inspiration

STYLE.COM
www.style.com

NET-A-PORTER
www.net-a-porter.com

PINTEREST
www.pinterest.com

JAK & JIL
www.jakandjil.com

YOUTUBE
www.youtube.com

INDEX

THANK YOU

To our families: this book is dedicated to you.

To *Jenny Duong* at **asos** for supplying us, without question, a box-full of DIY victims, twice!

To *Kate Pollard* at *Hardie Grant (UK)* for endless patience and golden guidance.

To *Jennifer Loiselle*, for the bridge that allowed all this to happen.

Susie Young and *Claire Knill* at *Knot & Pop* for the props that our beads and buttons now like to call home.

To my agent, *Abi Omole*, for opening the doors of the apartment and the promise of making anything and everything happen – Shini

To *Sharonda Calhoun* for introducing us to the magical dungeon of props.

To my husband, *Macius*, for the room service of coffees and popcorn, and for keeping the bed warm on the days I'd crawl in at wee hours – Shini

To my mother, for all her prayers that shake my world - Shini

To my family, and especially my mum, whose extraordinary sewing skills were taught to me at a very young age – Kit

To *Shini*, for being my first friend in the blogosphere. Without you, this book would still be an idea – Kit

Ditto, man – Shini

Last, but not least, *loyal readers, fans and supporters of our blogs*, without whom we'd never have grown and developed.

ABOUT THE AUTHORS

KIT LEE

Born in Northern Ireland and raised in London, Kit Lee of Hong Kong origin, is a London-based freelance fashion stylist, creative consultant, photographer, and jack-of-all-creative-trades. Graduating from London College of Fashion nearly a decade ago, Kit is a keen fashion crafter with ten years' worth of sewing and dress-making experience. Her DIY projects have featured in *Company*, *Grazia UK* and its international editions, *Glamour US*, *Marie Claire Mexico*, *Farfetch.com*, *Editer.com*, music videos and many more. Kit now freelances for Asia-based luxury publications and advertising clients, as well as UK and European clients.

Style Slicker.com is a fashion and lifestyle blog that originally started out as a street-style blog in 2008 before it became a fully fledged visual-heavy fashion and lifestyle blog five years later. The blog covers various topics, including beauty, eatery, DIY, factory visits, travel and so on.

www.styleslicker.com

SHINI PARK

Born in Seoul, raised in Warsaw and now London-based, Shini Park is a graphic designer and writer behind the fashion blog *Park & Cube*. After graduating at Central Saint Martins, Park now works as a freelance web designer and photographer, while managing the blog full-time. Her work has been featured in the likes of *Vogue Brasil*, *Elle Collections*, *GQ Magazine UK*, *Grazia UK*, and *Harpers Bazaar Australia*.

Launched in November 2008, *Park & Cube* is a fashion and lifestyle blog, heavy in photography and personal stories. Topics include beauty, fashion, food, lifestyle and travel, with a keen emphasis on personal style. Shini also hosts occasional in-store events reared on DIY tutorials.

www.parkandcube.com

Adorn 2014 by Kit Lee and Shini Park

First published in 2014 by Hardie Grant Books

Hardie Grant Books (UK)
Dudley house, North Suite
34–35 Southampton Street
London WC2E 7HF

Hardie Grant Books (Australia)
Ground Floor, Building 1
658 Church Street
Melbourne, VIC 3121
www.hardiegrant.com.au

British Library Cataloguing-in-Publication Data. A catalogue record for this book is available from the British Library.

ISBN 978-1-74270-653-5

Publisher: Kate Pollard
Desk Editor: Kajal Mistry
Art direction and Design: Shini Park
Photography © Shini Park & Kit Lee
Colour reproduction: p2d

Printed and bound in China by 1010 Printing International Limited
10 9 8 7 6 5 4 3 2 1